When You Have a Visually Impaired Student in Your Classroom

A Guide for Teachers

SUSAN J. SPUNGIN, *Consulting Editor*

Contributors
Donna McNear
Iris Torres

With
Anne L. Corn
Jane Erin
Carol Farrenkopf
Kathleen Mary Huebner

AFB
PRESS

Printed in the United States of America

Library of Congress Cataloging-in-Publication Data
When you have a visually impaired student in your classroom : a guide for teachers / Susan J. Spungin, consulting editor ; contributors, Donna McNear ... [et al.].
    p. cm.
    ISBN 0-89128-393-5
    1. Children with visual disabilities--Education--United States. 2. Mainstreaming in education--United States. I. Spungin, Susan Jay. II. McNear, Donna.
    HV1626 .W488 2002
        371.91'16--dc21

                                                    2002016482

The American Foundation for the Blind—the organization to which Helen Keller devoted more than 40 years of her life—is a national nonprofit whose mission is to eliminate the inequities faced by the ten million Americans who are blind or visually impaired.

Contents

1 Where Do I Begin? 1

2 How Do I Work with a Student
Who Is Visually Impaired? 17

3 How Will the Visually Impaired Student
Work in the Classroom? 25

4 How Will the Visually Impaired Student
Get Around and Manage Activities
Outside the Classroom? 39

5 What Additional Instruction and Assistance
Does the Visually Impaired Student Receive? 51

6 What Special Devices
Will the Visually Impaired Student Use? 63

Appendixes
      A Common Visual Impairments 75
      B Organizations of Interest to Teachers 79
      C Suggestions for Further Reading
         and Reference 85

About the Contributors 87

Writing and reading on a braille notetaker with refreshable braille.

1 Where Do I Begin?

You have just learned that you will have a visually impaired student in your class this year. Perhaps the student is totally blind or can use some vision to get around or to do schoolwork. If you have never worked with a visually impaired student before, you may not know what to expect. This booklet is for you. It will help you understand

- what you need to know to work with a visually impaired student,

- how you can help the student feel comfortable in your classroom and do his or her best,

- how you can feel more comfortable, too,

- who the other professionals are who will work with you and your student,

- what additional skills the student may need to learn,

- what types of accommodations and modifications in the classroom can help the student,

- what types of special devices may be used by visually impaired students, and

- where to get additional information and assistance.

Students who are visually impaired are as unique and diverse as any other group of students. They come from every background, with the full range of academic and other abilities and a wide variety of challenges. They may or may not have additional disabilities. Just as you get to know the personalities, strengths, and needs of the other students in your class, you will have the chance to become aware of and sensitive to the individual needs and abilities of the student who is visually impaired. Each individual's visual abilities are truly unique because even people with the same visual impairment can experience different degrees of vision loss. So just as with academic abilities, it is also important to get to know a student's unique visual abilities and needs.

When a visually impaired student is enrolled in a general education class, careful consideration needs to be given to whether the student can function both academically and socially alongside his or her sighted classmates. A thorough assessment of the student's academic and social functioning is completed, an Individualized Education Program (IEP) is developed, and an educational placement is recommended on the basis of the student's needs. (This process is discussed in more detail in the section "IDEA: The Law.") Like other students, a student who is visually impaired gains skills, self-assurance, and independence when he or she is able to learn and grow in an appropriate educational program. Students vary widely in their ability levels, degree of visual impairment, and other disabilities, but in general should participate as fully as possible in all academic and nonacademic activities with their classmates. You can support this participation in a variety of ways.

THE ROLE OF THE CLASSROOM TEACHER

You may be wondering what will be expected of you as the classroom teacher of a student who is blind or visually impaired. When you have a student with a visual impairment in your classroom, you are in charge of that student's overall academic program, as you are for all your students. The other sections of this booklet give you information and suggestions about how to help your student learn, given his or her special needs. You will also be working with specialists who are colleagues who will act as resources to you and whose job is to help make the instructional program work efficiently for the student.

Your positive attitude toward the integration and education of the student who is visually impaired may be the most important factor in guaranteeing the success and acceptance of this student in your class and school.

In your work with your student, an important partner is the teacher who specializes in the needs of students with visual impairments. Under federal law, students who are visually impaired are required to receive special services from qualified personnel. Certified teachers of visually impaired students teach such skills as reading and writing in braille and making the best use of existing vision with or without special devices and also help the student learn concepts that are not easily accessible to him or her. The teacher of visually impaired students will explain how you can reinforce these lessons in your classroom and how to make your own lessons accessible to the visually impaired student. Another professional—known as an orientation and mobility (O&M) instructor—may teach the student how to get around independently through the use of special travel skills. The O&M instructor will also explain to you how to reinforce some of the skills taught during O&M lessons.

Together, you and the teacher of students with visual impairments can plan appropriate educational activities and prepare the classroom environment and educational materials. The teacher of students with visual impairments will help to obtain special materials that the student needs. However, collaboration will be important for both of you. For example, if the student needs books or worksheets in braille or large print, the teacher will have to receive the print versions either on disk or in printed format from you with sufficient time to create or obtain the alternate media. Planning ahead to make sure that these instructional materials are prepared in advance is crucial so that they are available to the student at the same time they are used by his or her classmates. These special materials will enable the student to participate in class and benefit from your instruction.

As the general education teacher, you are responsible for teaching the core curriculum— literacy, mathematics, science, social studies, music, art, and so forth; or, if you teach in secondary school, you may teach in only one content area. The teacher of visually impaired students does not duplicate what you teach, but teaches students who are visually impaired the knowledge and skills they need to participate in your classroom instruction. The teacher of visually impaired students instructs them in specialized areas and skills that are related to their visual impairments and are important for their educational success, such as braille reading and writing, the use of assistive devices (special devices that usually make use of computer technology; see "What Special Devices Will the Visually Impaired Student Use?"), O&M, and skills for independent living. In the visual impairment field, these areas are known as the *expanded core curriculum* (see "What Additional Instruction and Assistance Does the Visually Impaired Student Receive?" for more details.)

Some school districts assign paraeducators to assist in classrooms where there are students with disabilities, or you may already have a classroom paraeducator as part of your program. In either case, clear directions must be given to the paraeducator to supplement—not substitute for—your role as the instructor teacher or that of the teacher of students who are visually impaired. In general, the paraeducator should be encouraged to work with small groups of students, rather than with the student who is visually impaired alone, to promote integration rather than separation within the classroom. "Roles and Responsibilities of Professionals Who Work with Visually Impaired Students in the Schools," at the end of this chapter, discusses in greater detail the primary professionals who work with visually impaired students.

You may also have occasional contact with other professionals who work with the visually impaired student, such as a physical therapist, speech-language therapist, or

4

adaptive physical education teacher. You may see reports on the student's health or vision from eye care professionals such as ophthalmologists, optometrists, or clinical low vision specialists. Other professionals who may work with visually impaired students include rehabilitation teachers, who can instruct them in skills related to personal care and independent living, and vocational rehabilitation counselors, who help visually impaired adolescents plan the transition from school to higher education, training, or work.

The next section discusses the services to which students with visual impairments are entitled under federal law. This booklet is intended to provide general education teachers with a basic understanding of how to be comfortable and effective working with visually impaired students, but it can only touch on a few topics. Additional resources are available for teachers who can use assistance or who want to go into more depth about some of these ideas (see "If You Need More Help . . .").

IDEA: THE LAW

Under federal law, students with visual impairments are expected to receive as much of their education as possible in a general education classroom following the regular curriculum, but they are also entitled to a variety of supports and services. As the student's general education teacher, you are part of a team that determines what those services should be and what modifications and accommodations the student needs in the classroom to help the student reach his or her educational goals.

The federal law governing the education of children with disabilities, including visual impairment, is the Individuals with Disabilities Education Act, or IDEA. Its most basic tenet is that children with disabilities must receive a "free appropriate public education in the least restrictive environment appropriate for that student." The least restrictive environment differs from student to student,

5

If You Need More Help . . .

If you need additional information or support, one place to begin is the office of the director of special education for your district. In addition, most states have the following agencies, which are primary sources of information:

- your state's special school for students who are visually impaired,
- the consultant from the state department of education who specializes in the education of students who are visually impaired, and
- the state commission for persons who are visually impaired.

To get specific contact information for your state, you can phone the American Foundation of the Blind (AFB) through its help-line number, 800-232-5463; consult the *AFB Directory of Services for Blind and Visually Impaired Persons in the United States and Canada*, available in many libraries; or access the organization's web site, www.afb.org.

In addition, the organizations listed at the end of this booklet offer information and assistance. The "Suggestions for Further Reading" provide both general information that can be shared with other students and parents and more in-depth discussions about various aspects of educating students who are visually impaired.

according to a student's abilities and needs and the skills the student has acquired during his or her school career. For some students, the least restrictive environment may be the neighborhood school with regular visits from a certified teacher of visually impaired students and an O&M instructor. Other students may be bused to a school where they receive several support services, including daily instruction from a teacher of visually impaired students and an O&M instructor, and participate in a resource room program. Still other students may attend a special school with or without residential programs during all or part of their school careers. To the extent possible, however, the student should be placed with his or her nondisabled peers.

The decision about which educational setting and services are most appropriate is a cooperative one based on the assessed needs of the student. An assessment and evaluation of the student's strengths and needs are conducted by an educational team consisting of the parent or guardian; a representative of the local educational agency; the teacher of visually impaired students; the O&M instructor; the student's general education teacher or teachers, the paraeducator (if one is assigned); related services personnel, such as a speech-language specialist; and, when appropriate, the visually impaired student. As part of this process, the team develops an IEP for the student. The IEP includes annual or long-term goals written as a guide to instruction, including specific goals that address the visually impaired student's educational needs. For each goal, there is a series of short-term objectives necessary to achieve the long-term goal. The teacher of visually impaired students may consult with both you and the student's family members before the IEP meeting about appropriate goals and objectives. During the meeting, all team members have the opportunity to provide further input into the goals and objectives so that they reflect a team consensus.

In addition to the support of the teacher of students who are visually impaired, students may be assigned other "related services"—support services that may include counseling, O&M, physical therapy, occupational therapy, and speech and language instruction, as well as other services to help students reach their IEP goals.

VISUAL IMPAIRMENT: SOME DEFINITIONS

Visual impairment generally refers to any visual condition that interferes with a person's ability to perform everyday activities. When you work with a visually impaired student, you may encounter a variety of related terms. Individuals who are not totally blind but have visual impairments that cannot be corrected to normal with regular eyeglasses or contact lenses are referred to as having *low vision*. *Functional vision* refers to the vision available to a person for the performance of everyday tasks; that is, how the individual uses his or her impaired vision in real-life situations. The term *blindness* generally refers to the lack of usable vision.

You may also encounter the term *legal blindness*, which was originally used to determine eligibility for public assistance programs, such as social security. This term refers to the visual ability of individuals who have a visual acuity of 20/200 or less in the better corrected eye (that is they can see at 20 feet what a person with normal vision sees at 200 feet) or who have a visual field of no greater than 20 degrees. The visual field is the area that can be seen without moving one's eyes when looking straight ahead: a visual field of about 160 to 180 degrees is considered typical. A restricted visual field (the inabiltiy to see peripherally) is often referred to as tunnel vision. Many students who are legally blind have a significant amount of usable vision; they often read regular or large print.

In this booklet, the term *visual impairment* is used to refer to a continuum of conditions, including blindness and low vision. Students who are classified as visually impaired may have a variety of eye conditions. Under IDEA, students are considered visually impaired if their vision condition, even after correction, adversely affects their educational performance.

Some students may have vision problems other than or in addition to reduced visual acuity or restricted visual field, including blind spots in their visual fields, high or low sensitivity to normal levels of light, difficulty distinguishing colors or contrast, or a combination of several of these conditions. (For more information on visual conditions, see Appendix A.) The type of visual impairment that a student has is also a major factor in his or her visual functioning. With some eye disorders, vision may actu-

8

ally fluctuate from day to day or throughout the day during different lighting and environmental conditions. Even stable visual conditions may be temporarily influenced by such factors as lighting, fatigue, attention, and emotions. In addition, many students have additional disabilities that accompany their visual impairments, such as cognitive impairments or learning disabilities.

It is essential to know that visually impaired students differ in their ability to use their vision. Two students may have the same visual acuity, visual fields, and other clinical measurements, but one may use sight to perform the same tasks that the other does more efficiently using his or her other senses. These individual differences affect the way the student obtains information and learns. The teacher of visually impaired students can discuss with you the specific needs or limitations of your student that are related to his or her visual impairment and can help determine the best ways in which to help your student learn.

Because students with different visual abilities are often placed in regular classes, this booklet makes suggestions that relate to visually impaired students overall. As was already indicated, many visually impaired students have more than one disability and thus also need to receive services from special education teachers with the appropriate expertise to meet their additional needs. They may be enrolled in your class for various amounts of the school day. Although educational strategies for students with multiple disabilities are not the main subject of this discussion, many of the suggestions presented here apply to them.

BASIC TIPS

Every student is a unique individual, and students who are blind or visually impaired are no exception. When you have a visually impaired student in your classroom, finding out about the student's visual as well as academic abilities and needs will be helpful to both you and the student. Reading the student's academic and other records and talking to his or her parents can provide you with a better understanding of the student and allow you to tailor instruction appropriately. The teacher of students who are visually impaired can help you understand any special requirements that the student has.

As you become acquainted with your visually impaired student, keep in mind the following basic guidelines:

- Remember that visual impairment is only one of your student's characteristics. He or she is a child first, with the same basic needs and desires of all children: the need to belong, to feel that there are high expectations, and to be successful. As with all children, some children who are visually impaired may be talkative and outgoing, and some may be quiet or shy. But they all deserve to be treated the same as the other children in class and to be held responsible for their behavior.

- When approaching or addressing a visually impaired student, always state your name unless he or she knows you well and can easily recognize your voice and encourage other students and adults in the school to do the same. Voices are not always easy to identify, particularly in crowds or during stressful situations. Discourage guessing games in which students or adults say, "Who am I?" or "You remember my voice, don't you?" Similarly, always let the student know when you are ending the conversation or walking away.

- Feel comfortable using words such as *see* and *look*. These words are as much a part of the vocabulary of visually impaired students as they are of the vocabulary of other students, particularly in such common expressions of everyday conversation as "See you later." Students with visual impairments also use these words to refer to their own methods of seeing or perceiving the world, such as by touching, hearing, or looking very closely.

- Introduce the visually impaired student as you would any student. When others ask questions about the student's visual impairment, you can encourage the student to answer them directly if he or she can. It is usually best to be open and honest about a visual impairment, and most visually impaired students will feel more comfortable when other students understand their visual limitations, as well as their strengths, talents, and interests. If the student seems uncomfortable discussing his or her visual impairment, a private conversation with the student or his or her parents or guardian may be helpful.

- It is also important to be sensitive and discreet and to respect the student's degree of adjustment to his or her visual impairment and level of comfort when discussing it with others. Some students may try to hide or deny their visual impairments, and others may not feel comfortable discussing visual problems in public. Some may simply consider their visual impairment to be a private matter. Conversations with the student, the teacher of visually impaired students, the O&M instructor, and the family may be helpful in knowing how to respond to inquiries from others.

- You need to describe for the student what others may see. For example, you may say, "I have made a chart to show every student's classroom job. It has a list of the jobs on one side and slots next to each job where we can put a card with the name of the student who is responsible for that task. Who can read the list of jobs out loud so we all know what they are?" Remember, too, that the visually impaired student may need more information than just, "Your seat is over there." Be specific: "Your seat is in the front row, two over from the window, next to Carla. I'll show you."

The sections that follow explain in more detail suggestions for working with students who have visual impairments, the types of accommodations and special skills that visually impaired students may use, and the strategies and approaches to use with a visually impaired student in your classroom. With an appropriate program, proper supports, and adapted materials—as well as effective communication and your ongoing help—a student who is visually impaired can thrive in your classroom.

Roles and Responsibilities of Professionals Who Work with Visually Impaired Students in the Schools

Many school personnel and other professionals may have occasion to work in school with students who are visually impaired, depending on the students' needs. However, certain professionals have primary responsibility for doing so: the student's general education teacher or teachers; the teacher of students who are visually impaired; and an orientation and mobility (O&M) instructor, if the student's IEP calls for instruction in this area. In addition, a paraeducator may be another staff person who works closely with the student.

The following outline summarizes the roles and general responsibilities of each of these professionals.

GENERAL EDUCATION TEACHER

- Teaches academic and social curricula for all students in the class, including the student who is visually impaired, and is responsible for grades and discipline for all students.
- Provides textbooks and instructional materials to the teacher of visually impaired students in a timely manner so the material can be prepared in alternate formats needed by the students, such as in braille, large-print, or an audio or electronic format.
- Communicates regularly with and schedules time to meet with the teacher of visually impaired students to discuss the student's progress and plans for meeting future educational and social needs.
- Creates a classroom climate that is comfortable for all students, including the student who is visually impaired.

12

- Serves on the team that prepares and monitors the student's IEP.

TEACHER OF VISUALLY IMPAIRED STUDENTS

- Teaches disability-specific skills and other aspects of the expanded core curriculum, including reading and writing in alternate media, such as braille or large print; the use of magnifiers and other optical devices; speech access software for the computer; and independent living skills.
- Conducts assessments of students who are visually impaired to determine their abilities and needs.
- Serves on the team that prepares and monitors the student's IEP.
- Prepares or obtains textbooks, instructional materials, and examinations in the appropriate accessible media (such as braille, large-print, audio, or electronic format) for use by students who are visually impaired at the same time as their classmates.
- Schedules time to meet with the general education teacher, family members, and other members of the educational team to discuss the student's progress and provide strategies for making the instructional environment accessible, including appropriate accommodations and adaptations.
- Provides suggestions and strategies to the general education teacher, family members, and other school personnel to include the student who is visually impaired to the greatest extent possible in all school, classroom, and extracurricular activities.
- Works with family members in various ways, such as helping them understand the development of students with visual impairments; helping them learn skills they need to teach their child; and facilitating the provision of appropriate recreational and rehabilitation services like camp activities and pre-employment experiences.
- Makes referrals for additional services, when necessary, such as for O&M instruction or clinical low vision services.
- Provides in-service training for teachers, paraeducators, and other school personnel on effective instructional strategies for teaching students with visual impairments.

O&M INSTRUCTOR

- Orients students who are visually impaired to the school environment.
- Teaches indoor and outdoor orientation and skills for safe and independent travel in the community.
- Consults with the general education teacher, the teacher of students who are visually impaired, school personnel, and family members to provide suggestions and strategies for reinforcing safe and independent travel skills.
- Teaches concepts about the body, space and direction, movement, and the physical environment.
- When appropriate, teaches students to use the long cane, optical devices, and/or their existing vision and other senses to move about the community independently, including crossing streets and traveling on public transportation.
- Provides in-service training to teachers, paraeducators, and other school personnel in orientation, the sighted guide technique, and other travel skills required by students who are visually impaired.
- Serves on the team that prepares and monitors the student's IEP.

PARAEDUCATORS

Some local educational agencies assign paraeducators (who are also called teachers' aides, paraprofessionals, school aides, or teaching assistants) to certain classrooms as part of particular programs. In some cases, paraeducators are assigned to classrooms in which there are students with disabilities to assist the general education teacher; in other cases, they are assigned to work with individual students who are visually impaired. In either situation, the paraeducator, with guidance from the teacher of visually impaired students, often does the following:

- Under the supervision of the general education teacher and with direction from the teacher of students with visual impairments and the O&M instructor, supports and reinforces classroom instruction.
- Prepares or arranges to obtain modified instructional materials and textbooks in braille, large print, or electronic or audio format.

14

- Helps students who are visually impaired practice skills that have been taught by the teacher of students with visual impairments and the O&M instructor.
- Works with a student who is visually impaired, following the instructions of the general education teacher and sometimes the teacher of students who are visually impaired or the O&M instructor, and encourages the student to complete assignments or tasks independently.
- Balances the need to maintain proximity to the student who is visually impaired for safety reasons with the need to maintain an appropriate distance to give the student the opportunity to interact socially with other students and adults and to develop independence and self-advocacy skills.
- Serves on the team that prepares and monitors the student's IEP.

When working with students who are visually impaired, it is important for paraeducators to resist providing too much assistance or supervision because doing so can interfere with the student's ability to develop independent skills.

Reading with a magnifier.

2 How Do I Work with a Student Who Is Visually Impaired?

In many ways, your work with a student who is visually impaired will be the same as with any other student. Although visually impaired students may need some assistance or special adaptations, most can complete all classroom work, get around the school and their community independently, and participate in all school activities. And it is important to realize that working with a visually impaired student can be not only challenging but immensely rewarding.

Some special needs of visually impaired students are more apparent than others. For example, because your gestures and expressions may not be readily apparent to this student or may not be visible at all, it is important to think about getting your messages across using your other senses besides sight; that is, emphasizing verbal, tactile, and other forms of communication. You may want to read a lesson aloud as you write it on the chalkboard and to provide opportunities for the visually impaired student to handle the materials during a science demonstration and explore them through the sense of touch. (See "How Will the Visually Impaired Student Work in the Classroom?" for more suggestions.)

In essence, working with a student who is visually impaired requires sensitivity to the unique ways in which he or she is able to gain access to information. The following suggestions will help both you and the student feel more comfortable and work more successfully in the classroom.

17

- Include the visually impaired student in all activities— physical education, art, science, family life science, computer instruction, industrial arts, technology education, and so on. In addition to the suggestions in this booklet, the teacher of visually impaired students and the O&M instructor can offer suggestions about the methods and special equipment or devices that may be helpful in performing some activities.

- Be aware that just as students from different backgrounds come into school with different experiences and knowledge about their world, students with visual impairments frequently may not have had as much access to information about their environment as some of their sighted peers. Their knowledge may be fragmented and incomplete because of their lack of visual information. Whereas sighted students can absorb concepts through incidental learning—such as through casual observation, pictures in books, and other visual experiences—visually impaired students may not have had the same opportunities to become aware of concepts with which they have not had direct experience. It is therefore important to be sensitive to possible gaps in what may otherwise be assumed to be common knowledge—for example, about concepts like farm animals (if the student lives in a city) or skyscrapers (if the student lives in a rural area).

- To promote independence, allow the visually impaired student to rely on himself or herself whenever possible. The student will also need to learn to ask for and accept assistance for certain tasks. In addition, to foster good peer interaction and a feeling of self-worth, the student should be encouraged to offer assistance to others.

- Like all students, students who are visually impaired are sensitive to teasing, criticism, or negative stereotyping from their peers. Your acceptance of the visually impaired student will provide a positive example for the class.

- Students with visual impairments may not be aware of, and therefore may not become interested in, events that are occurring at a distance. They may not notice, for example, a facial expression, nod, or arm movement suggesting that they come to their teacher or respond to a question. For some students with low vision, sitting near the front of the classroom can be helpful, as can verbal cues, such as calling the student by name.

- Encourage the visually impaired student to move about the classroom to obtain materials or visual information. The student will know his or her own needs, and his or her method of compensating will soon become part of the classroom routine. (See "How Will the Visually Impaired Student Get Around and Manage Activities Outside the Classroom?" for more information.) However, it is helpful for the student to be oriented to the classroom and for materials to be organized consistently in areas where the student can easily find them. You can consult the teacher of visually impaired students and the O&M instructor for suggestions in this regard.

- In relation to praise and discipline, the same disciplinary rules that apply to the rest of the class should apply to the visually impaired student. However, a smile of approval or encouragement is not always visible to a visually impaired student, so a verbal acknowledgment or a gesture, such as a pat on the back or shoulder, may serve as a substitute.

- Visually impaired students should be expected to do the same work as their sighted classmates, although they may need their materials in an adapted media (such as large print or braille) or sensitivity to time constraints. (See "How Will the Visually Impaired Student Get Around and Manage Activities Outside the Classroom?"

for more details.) As students develop visual or adaptive skills, their required workloads, time frames, and academic tasks should approximate those of the other students in your class and meet the same expectations; you and the teacher of students who are visually impaired should reexamine this issue from time to time.

- A student who is visually impaired may bring adaptive devices into the classroom. These devices may include a magnifier for reading print, a telescope for viewing the chalkboard, a computer with a braille display, or a portable braille notetaker, in addition to a mobility device, such as a cane (see "What Special Devices Will the Visually Impaired Student Use?" for more information). Some visually impaired students may wear tinted lenses indoors and outside or require special lighting. Encourage the student to use his or her adaptive devices as needed and to answer any questions that others may have about them.

- Because some visually impaired students prefer not to bring attention to themselves, they may use special devices and ask for assistance from others only when they have to. In general, you should respect the student's wishes, but if you suspect that a student really needs more assistance or that some other problem is developing, you may wish to discuss this concern with the teacher of visually impaired students or the O&M instructor.

- Provide additional work, desk, or locker space as needed to accommodate special materials that the student uses regularly, such as bulky braille or large-print books, optical devices, reading stands, computer systems, and scanners. Work with the student to make sure the space is convenient and well-designed. The student needs to learn to be responsible for his or her materials and keeping them organized.

- At times, all students like to hold positions of responsibility (to be team captain or program announcer or to take lunch money to the office, for example). Encourage the visually impaired student to compete for or accept leadership positions and classroom responsibilities just as the other students do.

- Students with visual impairments sometimes exhibit certain mannerisms, such as putting their fingers in their eyes (known as eye poking), rocking, making extra or rhythmic movements, drooping their heads, or making inappropriate sounds. Try to encourage the student to have good posture and consult with the teacher of students with visual impairments and family members about how to deal with any unusual behavior.

- Visually impaired students are sometimes unaware of social conventions of behavior because they have not been able to observe them consistently. If you notice that your student needs assistance in this area, encourage him or her to turn toward others when speaking with them, to maintain face-to-face contact or eye contact if able, and to respect local customs regarding body space and physical proximity.

- As a result of getting to know their classmate with a visual impairment, other students may become interested in topics related to vision and visual impairment. You may wish to incorporate these topics into your class lessons. In science, for example, light and optics may be a topic for discussion; in health, attitudes toward disabilities; in social studies, information about service agencies in the community and discrimination against persons with disabilities; in literature, books by and about people who are visually impaired. If the visually impaired student feels comfortable with this information, he or she may want to participate in the presentation of the lesson. However, since too much attention to the visual impairment may serve to emphasize differences, it is important to be sensitive to the need for balance in your discussions.

- Although he or she has special learning needs that must be addressed, the visually impaired student is much more like the other students in your class than he or she is different. Treating the student according to this principle will usually produce the best results for you, your student, and your class.

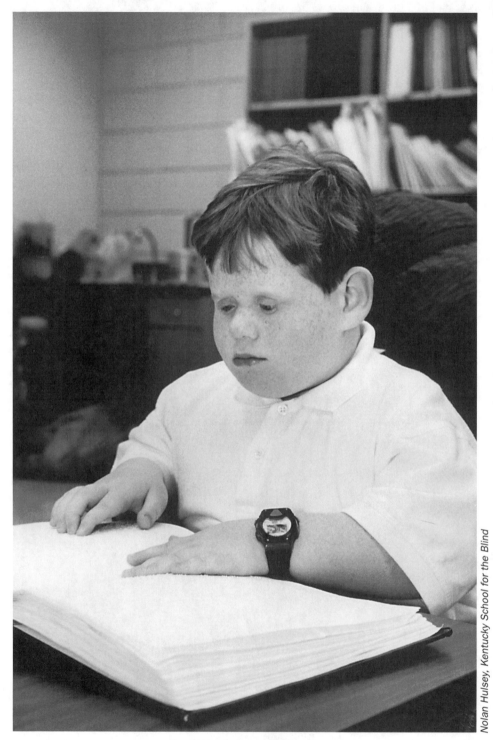

Reading braille.

3 How Will the Visually Impaired Student Work in the Classroom?

As you get to know your student, you will learn his or her ways of working and what changes or adaptations in the classroom or in your own teaching procedures will help the student to become fully integrated into your class. This section describes how students who are visually impaired typically work in class and presents suggestions for how you and your student can work effectively together. It is important whenever possible to collaborate closely with the teacher of students who are visually impaired, both to get his or her suggestions and to make sure he or she is aware in advance of any materials that will be needed, concepts that the student may need to learn, or any other preparations that are needed.

The ways in which an individual student works best are usually determined in the assessments conducted by the student's educational team and spelled out in the IEP. They include such issues as whether the student uses low vision devices; reads regular print, large print, braille, or some combination of these; is especially sensitive to light; is able to travel independently; and so forth. If you need additional information on these questions or other ways the student uses his or her vision, you can consult the teacher of visually impaired students, the student's records, family members, and the student. Sometimes it is necessary to try different options with a student for seating, obtaining written materials, and other classroom procedures to find what works best for him or her.

CHALKBOARDS, DRY ERASE BOARDS, AND OVERHEAD PROJECTORS

Where a student who is visually impaired is seated in the classroom can make a big difference in his or her ability to see what is going on. Location also affects the student's use of other senses, such as hearing and touch. The following suggestions will help visually impaired students follow lessons that are presented visually to the class using such media as chalkboards, dry erase boards, or overhead projectors.

- When the board is located at the front of the classroom, the front row center is sometimes a good place to seat a visually impaired student. However, if a student has a severely restricted visual field (tunnel vision), a seat farther back may be a better choice. The teacher of students who are visually impaired will be able to help identify the best seating arrangement for a particular student.

- Because glare may cause discomfort or interfere with their ability to read, some students with low vision (see the section on "Visual Impairments: Some Definitions") prefer seats that face away from the window. Others prefer seats close to the window to get more natural light and to avoid reflections off a shiny chalkboard or other surface.

- Encourage the student to use any prescribed low vision devices, such as telescopes, for distance viewing (see the section on "Optical Devices") from his or her seat. Some students who use telescopes prefer seats that are not too close to the chalkboard. It is important to work with the student to identify the best position for optimal viewing at different distances.

- Meet regularly with the teacher of students who are visually impaired to discuss what will be covered in class so that the teacher can prepare any needed materials in advance in alternate media, such as large print or braille. It is especially helpful to do so in mathemat-

Carol Farrenkopf

Using a monocular telescope

ics and other classes where it is necessary for students to follow step-by-step instructions.

- Lend the student with low vision a copy of the notes you put on the board or the book from which you have taken them so he or she can have time to read them. You can also e-mail a copy of your notes or give them to the teacher of visually impaired students to make a copy for the student in an accessible medium.

- When presenting a lesson, read the notes aloud as you are writing them on the board or projecting them on a transparency. The visually impaired student can follow the lesson auditorily or write the notes down as dictation.

- Consult with the teacher of students who are visually impaired for other ways in which you can help students with telescopic devices; those who have visual field defects; or those who may have special requirements regarding lighting, such as students with albinism.

- Some closed-circuit televisions (CCTVs) (see the section on "Assistive Technology Devices") allow students with low vision to read what is written on the board. These devices use a video camera to project a magnified image onto a television screen or computer monitor. If the CCTV is equipped with a special built-in camera that can swivel from distant objects to near objects, the student can focus on a chalkboard or chart at the front of the room and then refocus the CCTV to a near task.

DEMONSTRATIONS IN CLASS

The student's location in the classroom is also an important factor when you conduct class demonstrations. These suggestions will help the student get the most out of these educational experiences.

- If demonstrations are typically given during class, the location of the demonstrations should be taken into consideration when you assign permanent seats to students so that the visually impaired student can be seated in a location that maximizes his or her ability to see or follow what is being presented.

- When giving a presentation or lesson, avoid standing with your back to a window. When your back is toward a window, glare and backlighting will silhouette your figure, which may cause eye fatigue for some students with low vision. Cutting down on glare will benefit not only the visually impaired student but also the entire class.

- Allow the visually impaired student to stand or sit next to or to the side of any demonstration or use the student as a demonstration partner.

- Allow the student to handle the materials before or after the observation period or to assist in the demonstration (as an adaptation to accommodate the student's visual impairment, rather than as a special privilege).

- If feasible, provide a duplicate set of materials and have a classmate demonstrate the activity to the student who is visually impaired at the same time that the teacher is demonstrating.

- The teacher of students with visual impairments (or another member of the IEP team) may be able to demonstrate the activity being shown or "preteach" the prerequisite knowledge to the student before the classroom demonstration. For example, if there is going to be a demonstration of an eclipse of the sun, the teacher of students with visual impairments may teach concepts, such as shadow and revolution, beforehand.

- CCTVs equipped with a camera that can shift focus from distant objects to near objects, as described in the previous section, allow the student to view a demonstration at the front of the room.

TEXTS AND OTHER BOOKS

The student's method of reading should be specified in his or her IEP. Teaching a student to read in braille or to use low vision devices for reading is the responsibility of the teacher of visually impaired students (see "Braille Reading and Writing"). However, many visually impaired students can use books with regular-size type. They may need to bring the books closer to their eyes; use optical devices, such as magnifiers; and alter the position of the reading material so they can see it better. They may also require more time to complete their assignments (see the section on "Homework, Tests, and Reproduced Materials").

- If a student reads more efficiently with books in large print, braille, or electronic or audio formats, the teacher of visually impaired students will obtain them. As was already noted, students who are visually impaired use combinations of different modes of reading and writing. Again, it is important for you to give assignments

Braille: A Touchy Subject

General education teachers are sometimes confused about how they can teach a student who reads and writes in braille, when they don't know the braille alphabet themselves! However, braille instruction is the responsibility of a specialized teacher who is trained to work with visually impaired students. The division of labor that is both appropriate and effective is outlined below. Basically, teaching reading and writing in braille is the responsibility of the teacher of visually impaired students, but the general education teacher also has an important role in reinforcing that instruction all day. Here are some responsibilities each teacher has in this area:

TEACHER OF VISUALLY IMPAIRED STUDENTS

- Conduct an assessment of the best reading and writing medium for the student to make sure braille is appropriate.
- Instruct the student in braille reading and writing.
- Ensure that books and classroom materials are available in braille.
- Label classroom items in braille for beginning students.
- Select instructional materials that complement classroom activities.
- Make sure that the classroom teacher receives a print copy of assignments that the student completes in braille.

GENERAL EDUCATION TEACHER

- Participate in the IEP team's assessment and discussion of selecting braille as a reading and writing medium for the student.
- Collaborate with the teacher of visually impaired students to select instructional materials for literacy activities.
- Get written materials that the class will be using to the teacher of visually impaired students for brailling as early as possible.
- Make sure that the student reads and writes in braille throughout the school day.

and a list of required textbooks to the teacher of visually impaired students as far in advance as possible. If you know you are going to have a student with a visual impairment in your class, you will want to give a complete list of the books you use in your classroom to the teacher over the summer, before the student actually enters the class.

- In the upper grades, students may request their own braille, recorded, electronic, or otherwise adapted texts and other materials through such organizations as Recording for the Blind and Dyslexic, the American Printing House for the Blind, and the National Library Service for the Blind and Physically Handicapped (see "Organizations of Interest to Teachers" at the end of this booklet). Some school districts also hire braille transcribers. The teacher of visually impaired students can provide information in this regard.

WRITING IN THE CLASSROOM

The medium in which the student will write should also be specified in his or her IEP. You will want to consult with the teacher of visually impaired students to coordinate how the student will learn to write or complete written assignments, depending on his or her level, in your class. The following tips will be helpful in making it easy for a visually impaired student to write.

- Students with low vision may use bold-line paper, felt-tip pens, and other tools that increase the contrast and/or size of their writing to make it more visible.

- Students with low vision may benefit from using a reading stand or another method for bringing the paper closer to their eyes, rather than bending over a desk.

- Students with low vision may need to look very closely to learn to form letters but may not need to look as closely when they are writing.

- Students with low vision may initially write larger than their classmates, but many can, with practice, reduce the size of their letters. However, they will need to write in a size that they are able to reread.

- Students who are blind or who have low vision should be expected to take their own notes in class. Some will learn to take dictation when a teacher is reading aloud as he or she is writing on a chalkboard; others will be able to use optical devices to read and copy what is written on a chalkboard, transparency, or dry erase board.

- Students who learn to read and write in braille may use a braillewriter or a slate and stylus to write (see "What Special Devices Will the Visually Impaired Student Use?"). When the student needs to hand in written assignments, the teacher of students who are visually impaired may write the print words above the braille (known as interlining) so that you can read it. He or she should write exactly what the student brailles without correcting any errors so that you can get a true picture of the student's knowledge and writing skills.

- Some students may use other special devices, such as laptop computers or braille notetakers, to take class notes (see the section on "Assistive Technology Devices" in "What Special Devices Will the Visually Impaired Student Use?"). Braille notetakers are small portable computers with a braille keyboard that give speech or large-print output or both. (If the student uses speech output, he or she can use earphones so classmates are not disturbed.) Students who write class notes and assignments in this manner can save them to output later in braille if they use it or to copy to a home computer. These devices are also used to complete assignments that can be printed later on an ink-print printer and handed in to you.

- Students who are blind and learn to read and write in braille still need to learn to write their signatures. Students may also choose to learn to write the script alphabet using a raised-line drawing board or other instructional materials (see "What Special Devices Will the Visually Impaired Student Use?").

HOMEWORK, TESTS, AND REPRODUCED MATERIALS

It is essential that visually impaired students obtain the same information and materials as the other students in your class. For this reason, consulting with the teacher of students who are visually impaired about how to have materials prepared in advance for your student is critical. Some visually impaired students may read print, some may read braille, others use a combination of the two, and still others use audiotapes. In addition, students will increasingly make use of materials in electronic formats to be read on computers. The teacher can discuss with you the size and clarity of the type that a student who reads print will need (if enlarged type is necessary at all). The following suggestions may be helpful when you have a student in your class who is totally blind or a student with low vision who finds reprints unclear or difficult to read, even with the use of special optical devices.

- As far ahead of time as possible, give copies of materials to the teacher of visually impaired students to put into large print or braille, in electronic format, or on an audiocassette tape. It is also helpful if you give the visually impaired student assignments, especially long-term projects and reports, as far in advance as possible. Advance notice will allow time for any special ordering of materials or for locating personal readers who will read the information aloud to the student.

- Most schools have copiers with enlargement capabilities that can be used to enlarge tests and other handouts that are in regular-size print for students who need larger print. (Material that is prepared on a computer

33

can be printed out in a larger font.) When the material is enlarged, special attention should be given to clarity and contrast. However, students who use an optical device (see What Special Devices Will the Visually Impaired Student Use?) to read regular-size print materials should be encouraged to do so.

- For students who are competent computer users (see the section on Assistive Technology Devices in "What Special Devices Will the Visually Impaired Student Use?"), providing tests, assignments, and other reading material in electronic format may be preferable. Students have the advantages of completing answers directly on a question sheet, reviewing questions and spelling independently (through speech or braille), proofreading their own work by printing out the material in braille or large print, and keeping a copy in whatever format they wish.

- Providing "text-only" versions of any worksheets, tests, or other instructional materials prepared on a computer—reducing the use of or eliminating decorative graphics and other nonfunctional format features from the document—will make it easier to convert to braille or large print.

- Students who are visually impaired frequently need extra time to complete assignments and exams. In general, it is usually considered acceptable for students with low vision to take time and a half and for those who read braille to take twice the time. Time accommodations should be based on a student's reading speeds and stamina and written into the IEP. Some students prefer to take exams and complete assignments in a resource room to benefit from appropriate accommodations that have been agreed upon and are designated in the IEP.

- When you are certain that the student understands the work being studied, it may be appropriate to shorten the assignments. For example, you may request that a student do only the odd-numbered or more difficult problems in the math homework. These allowances need to be balanced with the amount of work that students in the class are expected to complete. Once a visually impaired student develops the necessary adaptive skills, your expectations should approximate those for other students. Remember that students who are visually impaired will eventually be competing with sighted peers in higher education and in the job market, so it is to the students' disadvantage to allow them to do less than their best effort.

- Consult the student's IEP for any specific modifications required for formal testing situations, such as extended time, an alternate test-taking setting, the use of assistive technology devices, special lighting, an alternate format, or the use of a tape recorder for responses. Make sure to inform the teacher of visually impaired students at the beginning of the year about any standardized examinations that your students will need to take so he or she can make arrangements to obtain them in alternate formats if necessary. You may also want to notify the person in your school or district who coordinates testing about standardized tests that you are going to need in braille or large print.

- Although you may be using separate answer sheets for the rest of the class when you are giving a test, it is usually easier for the visually impaired student to answer directly on the test. Answer sheets with "bubble" responses or empty sets of parentheses to be filled in, such as those used in standardized tests, may cause problems for a visually impaired student. Substituting an answer sheet on which the student circles the correct a, b, c, or d answer will also eliminate the problems involved in filling in difficult-to-see bubbles. For exams in braille, however, separate answer sheets may be needed, even though the class edition requires responses directly on the test. Before a testing period, consult with the visually impaired student or the teacher of students with visual impairments for the best method to use.

- A classmate, the teacher of students with visual impairments, or the paraeducator can write down test answers that the visually impaired student gives orally. A tape recorder, which allows for more independent responses, may also be used for this purpose. However, this method does not allow the student to review his or her answers as sighted students are able to do. Some students will type their answers using a laptop computer or portable notetaker.

- In general, consult with the teacher of students who are visually impaired to determine the most appropriate modes of reading and writing for a student and how different tasks may require him or her to select alternative modes.

MAPS AND CHARTS

- The teacher of students with visual impairments may have maps enlarged or otherwise modified for the student's use. He or she may need to simplify maps or diagrams that are visually complex for ease in viewing or to make them comprehensible in a tactile format.

- You may want to give a desk copy of a chart or map that is displayed in the classroom to a student with low vision to look at up close.

- Raised maps (on which the lines or areas are raised so that they can be perceived tactilely) or "sound maps" (which are recorded descriptions) may be used with students who are visually impaired.

- The teacher of students with visual impairments may work with the student before the class lesson, especially if the student needs to explore a map tactilely and create a mental image of the information presented.

FILMS, VIDEOS, AND MULTIMEDIA PRESENTATIONS

- Arrangements may be made with the teacher of students who are visually impaired to show a videotape, film, or other multimedia presentation to the visually impaired student before or after the class has seen it to ensure that the student has understood all the visual concepts presented.

- A classmate, teacher, or paraeducator can narrate or describe the video, film, or multimedia presentation to the student, depending on the content.

- Some videos are available with a narrative description already recorded as part of the video's sound track (audio description). The teacher of students who are visually impaired will have information about obtaining such materials.

- When you are showing a video with subtitles, ask one of the students to read the titles aloud to the class.

- The person who is responsible for audiovisual material in a school or school district can be a resource for ideas and devices to be used in the classroom.

Readers should note that the tips presented here are useful for most general classroom work. Some subjects, such as science, mathematics, or art, may require additional adaptations or modifications to help students who are visually impaired participate with their classmates. Although an in-depth discussion of these areas is beyond the scope of this booklet, you can consult the teacher of students who are visually impaired or the resources at the back of this booklet for more information.

Coming in from recess.

4 How Will the Visually Impaired Student Get Around and Manage Activities Outside the Classroom?

Many students who are visually impaired will not have difficulty moving around the classroom and traveling from place to place in school once they are familiar with the environment. The teacher of students who are visually impaired or the O&M instructor will familiarize a student who is visually impaired with the classroom and surrounding area and instruct the student in how to get to and from the classroom independently (see the following section on O&M Instruction). The specialists will alert you if any specific areas (such as stairs, an outside playground, or dimly lighted areas) may cause problems.

The following are some general points to remember about assisting your student to move about the school safely and independently:

- When giving the visually impaired student directions, be as specific as possible. Try to keep in mind that the student may not be able to see what you do and provide descriptions accordingly. For example, say, "The new learning center is in the back of the room to the left of the computer" and give specific directions to get there, rather than just saying "It's over there."

- Sometimes students develop a better understanding of their position in space through distinct environmental features, such as differences in the textures of floor coverings. For example, feeling a rug underfoot may let the student know that he or she is in the reading center. It is important to secure area rugs and other floor coverings so they do not slip.

- For the safety of the visually impaired student, as well as of all other students, keep doors and cupboards either completely closed or completely open. Classmates need to push their chairs all the way in when they are not seated at their desks. The visually impaired student should also be told of any changes in the position of classroom furniture from those with which he or she is familiar.

- Visual contrast in the environment can assist students who have low vision. For example, placing a strip of high-contrast colored tape on the floor can indicate a change in the level of the traveling surface, such as a ramp or step.

- Labeling the student's belongings contributes to the student's independence in being able to find his or her own place and possessions. Label the student's locker, shelf, box, or other places the student uses frequently. Depending on the student's visual ability and reading skills, the labels can be large print; braille; or other tactile or visual symbols, such as a crayon taped to the student's supply box or a mitten on a young student's coat cubby. (The teacher of students who are visually impaired can help with braille and other special labels.) Older students will be able to create labels on their own.

- Under IDEA regulations, students ought to be assessed for their travel needs as part of their educational program planning (see the following section on O&M Instruction. Stay informed about your student's progress in learning to travel independently and to use mobility devices, such as a long cane. Become familiar with the student's IEP, discuss its components with the teacher of visually impaired students, and encourage the student to use his or her travel skills and mobility devices as appropriate to the student's educational plan.

O&M INSTRUCTION

Depending on the nature of his or her visual impairment, your student may need instruction in special travel techniques and skills. A person whose visual impairment is severe enough to affect his or her ability to get around learns to travel safely and confidently through instruction in O&M. *Orientation* refers to the ability to know where one is in the environment, and *mobility* refers to the ability to travel safely and independently using various techniques or assistive devices, including

- becoming familiar with the environment

- using a hand to trail along the walls of a room or hallway

- using a white cane or other mobility devices

- walking with a sighted guide

- following a teacher or another student, using the other person's movements as visual cues

O&M is identified as a "related service" under IDEA. That is, it is a support service that may be necessary for students with visual impairments to enable them to travel safely and to benefit from other instruction. O&M is taught by an instructor who is specially trained and certified in these skills. Although teachers of students who are visually impaired can provide some instruction in basic O&M skills, such as the sighted guide technique (see the following section) and indoor travel techniques, O&M instructors have the extensive training, knowledge, and skills to teach students the full range of O&M techniques, including advanced travel skills in outdoor environments.

The decision to provide O&M instruction is based on the needs, goals, and objectives identified in the student's educational planning process. The O&M instructor will assess the student's needs, orient the student to his or her classrooms and other areas of the school, and teach the student routes for traveling around the school and community. O&M instruction may include the development of sensory and motor skills; the formulation of concepts about the environment; instruction in following directions, crossing streets, and using public transportation; and lessons in using special mobility aids, such as canes, tactile and auditory maps, compasses, and electronic travel devices. If you think your student needs additional mobility instruction, consult with the teacher of visually impaired students and the student's IEP team.

SIGHTED GUIDE TECHNIQUE

A visually impaired person may travel with the assistance of another individual using a method called the *sighted guide* or *human guide technique*. The teacher of students with visual impairments or O&M instructor will demonstrate these sighted guide techniques to you if it is a method the student uses for travel.

The following are some basic principles of the sighted guide technique:

- The student grasps the guide's upper arm firmly, just above the elbow, so that the thumb is on the outside and the fingers are on the inside of the guide's arm (a younger student walking with an adult may hold the adult's wrist). Both the student and the guide hold their upper arms close to their bodies, so the student is automatically positioned one-half step behind the guide and can follow the movement of the guide's body.

- When narrow passageways are being negotiated, the guide's arm can either be pressed closer to the guide's body or placed behind the body so that the student knows he or she must move directly behind the guide.

42

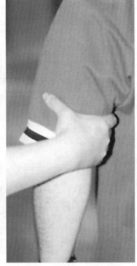

Nora Griffin-Shirley

(Left) Sighted guide technique: walking half a step behind the guide. (Center) Grasping the guide's elbow with the hand in a cupped position. (Right) Moving behind the guide to negotiate a narrow passageway.

- Verbal cues are also important. The guide should inform the student when they have reached any point or obstacle requiring a change in direction, level, or speed, such as a stairway or a curb.

- The guide should approach changes in levels squarely, never at an angle. The guide ascends or descends the first step, and the student follows one step behind.

- When reaching a landing, the guide should take one step forward and then stop as a cue to the student who is one step behind that there is one last step.

- As the student and the guide become more familiar with each other, a full pause by the guide with feet together may be sufficient to indicate an approaching change in level without verbal cues.

O&M DEVICES

An O&M instructor may teach a student to use one or more of the following devices:

- **The long cane.** The long cane is the traditional device used for safe, efficient, and independent travel. It is used to detect obstacles or drop-offs (such as curbs or stairs), gather information, and provide protection from low-lying objects.

- **Optical devices.** A number of prescription optical devices are used to help students with low vision make the best use of their sight. (For more details, see "What Special Devices Will the Visually Impaired Student Use?") *Telescopes,* which enlarge images of objects, are used for detecting and seeing details of distant objects and signs in the environment and for such tasks as finding and reading street signs and bus numbers. *Reverse telescopes,* which make objects appear smaller, may be used to expand the amount of information in the student's visual field. *Magnifiers* enlarge images and assist with such tasks as reading maps and bus schedules for independent travel.

- **Precane or alternate mobility devices.** Precane devices are sometimes used with young students or students with additional disabilities to assist them with beginning independent travel skills. They range from devices like push toys to instructor-made devices from PVC pipe that students can use to maneuver safely through the environment. Devices are also specially designed for students who use wheelchairs.

- **Braille or talking compass.** Specially modified compasses exist that can be used tactilely or that have sound output. These devices inform students about their location and assist in orientation skills.

- **Tactile maps and other wayfinding systems.** The O&M instructor may make or provide large-print or tactile maps (with raised lines and other textured surfaces that can be felt) of the school, the community, shopping malls, or other environments. Depending on the age and skill of the student, the O&M instructor may also decide to introduce "talking" street atlases on computer disk or web sites that describe locations using sound output.

SAFETY

A frequent concern of general education teachers is the safety of visually impaired students. Although certain precautions must sometimes be taken, it is important to remember that safety practices must be balanced with a student's need to be independent. However, some students may prefer not to participate in certain activities; for example, a student with low vision may find it difficult to participate in games that require visually tracking a fast-moving ball.

Consult with the teacher of students with visual impairments or the O&M instructor about a student's participation in class activities or any extra safety precautions you are considering with physical education and other activities, including the use of machinery. Some of the suggestions in this section may be helpful for safety in and around the school building and outdoors.

The O&M instructor or teacher of students who are visually impaired will orient the student to areas in and around the school building. He or she will teach the student travel and self-management strategies in using bathrooms, locating drinking fountains, locating and using the student's locker, negotiating the hallways and stairways, and other situations that are necessary for independence and safety. As a student makes progress in developing independent travel and self-management skills in such settings as the lunchroom, the general education teacher can have an important role in encouraging the student to use new skills as they are learned.

Fire Drills

- The subject of fire drills and other possible emergencies should be discussed with the class as a whole. The other students and adults in the class should become familiar with the sighted guide technique used to guide the visually impaired student.

- The visually impaired student should be instructed to travel with another student or adult using the sighted guide technique during a fire drill and to follow the others quickly and quietly. Assigning only one sighted student the job of being the visually impaired student's regular guide in such situations may be ineffective because the assigned student may be absent or elsewhere.

- Practicing the fire drill route in and out of the school ahead of time with the O&M instructor or the teacher of students who are visually impaired should help reduce the potential stress and dangers inherent in a surprise fire drill or actual fire. It is essential for the visually impaired student to know the emergency escape routes from all areas of the school.

- It is advisable to consult with the teacher of students who are visually impaired, the O&M instructor, and school administrators regarding fire and other emergency evacuation procedures.

Auditorium

- The student may choose to sit close to the stage and should be allowed to do so. Some students may feel more comfortable sitting up front if they are allowed to choose a friend to sit with. An aisle seat may also be appropriate for safety reasons or for students in wheelchairs.

- The student may need to sit in an appropriate location for using a telescopic device for distance viewing.

Lunchroom

- An initial orientation to the lunchroom by the O&M instructor or the teacher of students who are visually impaired may be necessary so that the visually impaired student learns where trays are located, where lines form, and so forth. At the beginning of a new semester or school year, the student may need assistance in finding a seat. Other students or staff members may give the student physical assistance or verbal directions to get to an empty seat until the student develops a routine.

- It is advisable to alert counter workers so they can inform the student, if necessary, about the day's food selections. The cafeteria staff should also be asked to notify the student about unusual obstacles, such as mops and water buckets, or about changes in the organization of tables or the location of trash cans.

- It may take some time and practice for a totally blind student to coordinate his or her use of a cane and walking with a tray full of food. The O&M instructor will provide instruction in this area.

Physical Education and Other Special Classrooms

- Most students who are visually impaired should participate fully in physical education activities. However, students with certain conditions, such as a potential for retinal detachment, may have restrictions placed on their participation by their health care providers. In such cases, a note from the physician should be in the student's file, and the restriction should be noted in the IEP.

- The teacher of students who are visually impaired can collaborate with the physical education teacher on appropriate modifications that will allow the student to participate fully and actively in physical education programs. Participation in specific classroom activities like using power tools should be discussed with the IEP team, which should determine appropriate modifications. The teacher of students with visual impairments can recommend safety techniques and equipment.

- The student may benefit from an initial orientation by the O&M instructor or teacher of students who are visually impaired to special classroom settings, such as a gymnasium, wood shop, auto shop, or family life science classroom.

Playground and Outdoor Recess

- The O&M instructor should give the student an initial orientation to the outdoor environment of the school. He or she can alert the student to safety concerns about playground equipment, such as traveling near swings.

- Recess provides an excellent opportunity to develop social relationships, and the regular education teacher can help by encouraging visually impaired students to participate. Strategies for participation can be discussed with the student's IEP team.

TRIPS

- Trips are especially worthwhile for visually impaired students because they can provide real-life experiences that enhance and reinforce instruction and promote the development of concepts about the world.

48

- When visiting a theater, museum, or other exhibit, you may want to notify someone on the staff that a visually impaired student will be present. If the staff are told in advance, they may be able to make arrangements for the student to go beyond the museum barriers or to touch some of the exhibits. They may also be able to make audiodescribed, taped, or brailled materials available to the student.

Teaching braille to a beginning student.

5 What Additional Instruction and Assistance Does the Visually Impaired Student Receive?

All students, disabled and nondisabled alike, participate in a school's core curriculum. This curriculum typically consists of all the subjects taught in school, such as reading, mathematics, science, social studies, and physical education. However, because students with visual impairments need to learn a range of adapted techniques and alternate ways of doing everyday activities like reading, writing, and traveling independently, they need to develop certain essential skills. These skills are taught as part of a specialized and vital area of study known as the expanded core curriculum.

EXPANDED CORE CURRICULUM

The expanded core curriculum consists of subjects that are specific to the learning needs of students who are visually impaired. These subjects, which are addressed by the teacher of students with visual impairments and the O&M specialist, include

- compensatory or functional academic skills, including communication modes (such as braille reading and writing)
- O&M skills

- social interaction skills

- independent living skills

- recreational and leisure skills

- career education

- use of assistive technology

- visual efficiency

Students who are visually impaired need to be assessed in all the areas of the expanded core curriculum to identify their individual needs for instruction in each area.

The following discussion briefly explains the areas of the expanded core curriculum and gives examples of specific skills that the teacher of students who are visually impaired may teach your student.

Compensatory or Functional Academic Skills and Communication Modes

Compensatory skills include many basic skills that visually impaired students need to have access to information that sighted people usually obtain visually. They are the skills needed to participate fully in their general education subjects—the core curriculum—as well as general communication skills. *Functional academic skills* refers to the skills needed to accomplish daily living tasks, such as reading signs or paying bills. *Communication modes* refer to the methods of reading and writing that students use for literacy tasks, such as braille reading and writing.

Concept Development

Students who have been visually impaired since birth or from the first few years of life must be taught concepts that sighted children develop as a matter of course. For example, they may need to learn such spatial concepts as above, below, and next to in relation to themselves and others and may need to develop a sense of how the individual parts of an object actually constitute a whole. Older students may have difficulty understanding the concepts of rotation and revolution. Spatial and environmental concepts are usually taught as part of O&M instruction. Visually impaired students also need concrete educational experiences, which the teacher of students with visual impairments may help plan and reinforce, that offer them the opportunity to explore objects and their environment thoroughly using senses other than sight and to learn by doing.

Braille Reading and Writing

Students who are totally blind typically use braille as the medium of written communication just as sighted children use print. And, as with print, learning to read and write braille is a gradual process that involves constant practice and much trial and error. Beginning braille readers need daily instruction from a teacher of visually impaired students, who also provides the braille materials a student needs to participate in classroom learning activities. Various methods can be used to obtain print copies of the student's braille assignments so you can read and correct the student's work. Sometimes the teacher of visually impaired students writes in print above the student's braille writing (interlining). When available, various electronic tools, such as electronic braillewriters, braille notetakers, and braille translation software can provide access to the student's assignments (see the section on "Assistive Technology Devices"). Some regular classroom teachers are interested in learning to read and write braille; the teacher of students with visual impairments can provide information on how to learn the braille code.

Print Reading and Writing

Students with low vision may read regular-print text with or without the help of optical and nonoptical devices (see "What Special Devices Will the Visually Impaired Student Use?") or use large-print materials. In some cases, they may also use braille. It is up to the IEP team (based on its assessment and the recommendations of a clinical low vision specialist) to determine the best way for a student to gain access to print information; whether the student needs any modifications, such as bold-line paper, for writing; and whether the student needs instruction in how to use optical and nonoptical devices for efficient reading.

Listening

Listening skills enable children who are visually impaired to make efficient use of the sense of hearing. These skills are particularly important for listening to recorded texts and obtaining information from teachers' presentations and class discussions. Tuning into sounds in the environment is also essential for the development of O&M skills. Listening skills taught by the teacher of students who are visually impaired and the O&M instructor supplement those taught in the regular classroom.

Study and Organizational Skills

Study and organizational skills are critical because visually impaired students need to manage many tasks, materials, files, and information to live independent lives. Students need instruction in organizing books, papers, electronic information, and important resources and may also need help in developing study skills, such as taking notes, skimming materials for information, using reference materials, writing drafts of written work, and conducting research. Classroom teachers can reinforce good study skills by expecting students to be responsible for their own materials, assignments, and due dates and by expecting them to take notes.

O&M Skills

The ability to move about safely, effectively, and independently is a fundamental need. Students who are visually impaired learn to do so through O&M instruction in basic body image, spatial concepts, sensory awareness, and a variety of travel skills in indoor and outdoor environments. Students also learn techniques such as self-protection skills, sighted guide, and cane travel skills (see "How Will the Visually Impaired Student Get Around and Manage Activities Outside the Classroom?").

Social Skills

The ability to interact with other people is an essential part of daily life. From maintaining eye contact to greeting people with a handshake, social interchanges form the foundation of personal and business relationships. When a student's visual impairment interferes with the observation and imitation of social behaviors, such as nonverbal communication like facial expressions and body language, it may be necessary for the teacher of students with visual impairments to provide focused instruction. You can also encourage the student to interact socially by involving him or her with others whenever possible and by alerting the teacher of visually impaired students to any additional social skills that you observe the student needs to learn. Students should be encouraged to develop appropriate behavior, such as looking at or toward the person they are speaking to, offering their hand during introductions, and taking turns speaking in a conversation.

Independent Living Skills

Essential for the development of independence and a feeling of self-worth, daily living skills include the how-tos of everyday life, from good grooming and hygiene to cooking a meal to organizing and locating belongings. All students need to learn such practical skills as how to shop for groceries and do laundry. These activities, which sighted students learn through incidental observation, may need to be taught to visually impaired students. For students with visual impairments, practical skills include not just performing tasks like making purchases, but arranging for assistance when it is appropriate. The teacher of visually impaired students will assist the visually impaired student in acquiring these practical skills, and you need to consult with this teacher about tasks that the student can learn to do independently (such as using a combination lock and assisting in classroom routines).

Recreational and Leisure Skills

The development of lifelong recreational and leisure skills is essential for visually impaired students. To participate in leisure activities, these students may need to develop adaptive techniques, as well as concepts like body awareness and spatial orientation. Students need to be exposed to and participate in a variety of sports, hobbies, and recreational activities, including card playing, board games, woodworking, sewing, boating, skating, bowling, golf, skiing, and the use of exercise equipment, to be aware of the opportunities that are available to them.

Natalie Isaak Knott

Learning daily living skills.

Visual Efficiency Skills

The teacher of students with visual impairments helps students discover the conditions under which they can most effectively use their vision, for example, what types of lighting, positioning of materials, and type size are best for them. When new eyeglasses or optical devices are prescribed, the teacher of students with visual impairments consults with the eye care specialist to discuss how the new device will affect the conditions under which a student should work. If you have any questions about how a student should be using a prescribed device, you can ask the teacher of students with visual impairments. The teacher of students with visual impairments and the O&M instructor also perform functional vision assessments to determine how a student uses his or her vision and conduct instructional programs needed to increase the student's visual efficiency and to determine which learning medium is most appropriate (braille, print, or both).

Career Education

Because people who are visually impaired have historically been unemployed and underemployed, career education is another critical area of the expanded core curriculum. Students who are visually impaired often do not understand what jobs people do or how they complete them because they cannot observe them doing so. They need concrete, real-life experiences and information on a wide variety of jobs and the specific tasks required to perform them. They also need to be exposed from an early age and throughout their education to actual work sites and places of employment.

Assistive Technology

Assistive technology refers to computer hardware and software and other equipment that give students who are visually impaired access to the same information and mainstream technology as sighted students. Visually impaired students need to be able to use a variety of assistive technology tools and computers to access electronic information and communicate with others.

Assessment and Instruction

The teacher of students who are visually impaired is responsible for assessment and instruction in the use of assistive technology that is specially designed for visually impaired students. (See the section on "Assistive Technology Devices" for a discussion of specific devices.)

Keyboarding

The ability to type rapidly and accurately on a computer keyboard is essential for all students but it is especially important for students who are visually impaired, for whom it can provide an alternative means of doing written assignments. Some visually impaired students find their own handwriting difficult to read, and the task of writing can be fatiguing or even nonproductive, depending on a student's functional vision. Instead, students can make use of personal computers that are modified so that the output is in voice, braille, or enlarged print (see the section on "Assistive Technology Devices").

Keyboarding and word-processing skills may be taught by the teacher of students with visual impairments, or the student may choose to participate in classes offered as part of the regular school curriculum. In general, computer-assisted instructional programs should be as available to visually impaired students as they are to sighted students in the classroom.

Translating Text into a Variety of Formats

Visually impaired students need to be able to translate text that they have accessed electronically into their appropriate reading medium. For example, a student can receive a worksheet created by the classroom teacher via e-mail or on a disk and access the worksheets in braille, speech, or large print by using appropriate translation software and hardware devices. Students who read and write in braille can also provide their sighted teachers with their work by translating their braille assignments into print.

OTHER SPECIAL EDUCATIONAL SERVICES

Assessment

In addition to regular assessment in the school's core curriculum, students who are visually impaired need to be assessed in all areas of the expanded core curriculum to ensure that their unique needs are met. It is important to include parents and all team members in the assessment process because the student's behavior and performance in all environments, including school, home, community, and recreational settings, should be evaluated.

IEP

As was mentioned earlier, the IEP is developed by all members of the student's educational team, including the student when it is appropriate. The IEP team assesses the student's present level of functioning in academic, physical, and social skills; identifies the student's needs in all areas of development; and develops annual goals and objectives based on the student's needs. The general education teacher has an important role as a team member in this process and provides a crucial perspective on the student's performance throughout the school day and in all school activities.

Materials

As was discussed in previous sections, special or adapted materials can be obtained for the student's use in a variety of formats. The teacher of students with visual impairments and the O&M instructor will help the student learn to obtain and care for the devices and equipment he or she uses.

Remedial Academic Assistance and Guidance

The teacher of students with visual impairments collaborates with the general education teacher and other educational team members to determine the visually impaired student's strengths and weaknesses in academic and nonacademic subjects. He or she can be helpful in locating appropriate tutors if such assistance is necessary. Students may have additional disabilities besides their visual impairment, such as a learning disability, that can be the source of academic or behavioral difficulties. If this is the case, a teacher specializing in this area should become part of the educational team.

An important part of the job of the teacher of students who are visually impaired is to provide an understanding atmosphere in which a visually impaired student can learn to deal with his or her feelings about the disability and to cope with the attitudes of others. He or she also maintains close contact with the student's parents or guardians to help them understand their child's development and other aspects of his or her situation. The school guidance department also shares the responsibility of personal counseling and career education.

Transition Planning

The transition from school to adult life is a critical passage for all students. Under federal law, transition IEPs need to be completed for visually impaired students aged 14 and older. High school students should also consult with a vocational counselor from the state agency or department concerned with the needs of visually impaired students, in addition to the school's guidance department. Students need to learn about their state's programs for vocational rehabilitation services and services available to teach additional independent living or O&M skills, if needed, and any financial assistance programs available for higher education and assistive technology.

The skills taught as part of the expanded core curriculum, as well as other special education services that visually impaired students may receive, are additional to the general education curriculum. They are necessary for visually impaired students to participate in school and complete their schoolwork. As the general education teacher responsible for a student's regular school subjects, discipline, and overall education, you can discuss these areas with the professionals who teach these skills and consult with them about how to best support your student in their use.

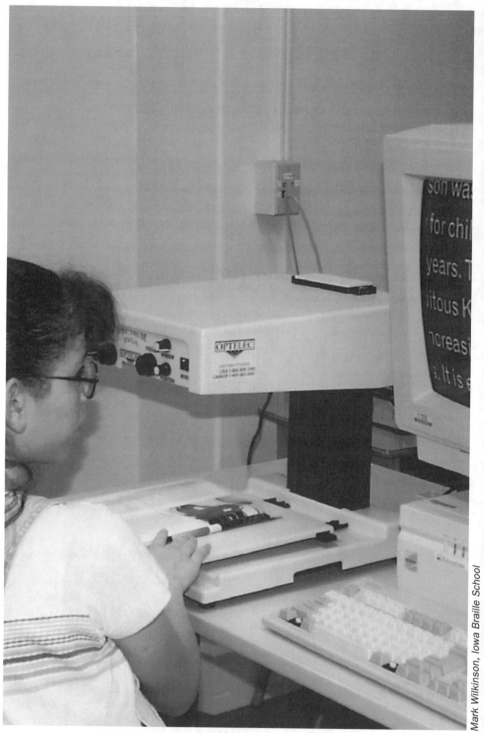

Using a closed-circuit television (video magnifier).

6 What Special Devices Will the Visually Impaired Student Use?

Students who are visually impaired may use a variety of equipment, devices, and tools to assist them with various academic and everyday tasks. Some students may need only a few adaptive devices, while others need to use several in combination.

These devices are generally categorized as optical devices, nonoptical devices, and assistive technology. The following sections describe each category and offer a partial list of devices. (See "How Will the Visually Impaired Student Work in the Classroom?" for information on other ways of assisting visually impaired students with their classroom work.)

OPTICAL DEVICES

Optical devices use lenses to optimize a person's existing vision. Some of the ways they do so are by enlarging or modifying a visual image, altering the apparent position of an object, controlling light, and changing the apparent size of the visual field. They are prescribed by a clinical low vision specialist, an opthamologist or optometrist who specializes in working with people who have low vision. The following are some types of optical devices:

- **Eyeglasses** with special prescriptions have two basic functions:
  —to improve vision, using bifocals, prism lenses, contact lenses, or other prescribed combinations of lens-

es for a student with low vision to be used at all times or only during specified activities, such as reading.

—to reduce glare or excess light, both indoors and outdoors, for a light- sensitive student using lightly tinted or dark lenses.

- **Magnifiers.** Magnifiers make objects appear larger by increasing the size of the image reaching the eye. They may be handheld, mounted in a stand that sits on top of the material to be viewed, or worn as a loupe over eyeglasses. Magnifiers may be used for such tasks as reading, writing, and artwork.

- **Telescopes.** Small telescopes are used to view objects at a distance, such as dry erase boards and class demonstrations, and can also be used during travel to identify buses, street signs, and so on. They can be either handheld or mounted in eyeglass frames.

NONOPTICAL DEVICES

Nonoptical devices are also used to assist visually impaired people to perform everyday tasks, but they do not involve lenses, may or may not be designed specifically for visually impaired students, and do not have to be prescribed by an eye specialist. These devices, many of which are listed in the following sections, may be intended to help visually impaired students make maximum use of their sight or to enhance their use of their other senses. The teacher of students with visual impairments or the O&M instructor will make recommendations about which of these devices may benefit a particular student.

Devices for Enhancing Visual Functioning

Many ordinary or easily available objects and devices can be used to assist visually impaired students to make better use of their existing vision.

- **Book stands.** When book stands are designed specifically for persons with low vision, they help reduce postural fatigue by bringing the work closer to the reader's eyes. When a book stand is not available, one may be improvised by placing books or a large binder beneath the book that is to be read.

- **Wide felt-tipped pens and markers.** Felt-tipped pens, available in various widths, produce a bold, high-contrast letter or diagram. They usually provide the most effective contrast in black, but the use of different-colored markers may help a student emphasize sections of his or her notes when scanning through them would otherwise be difficult. (Leaving a blank line between each line of text written may also make it easier for the student with low vision to read the material.)

- **Acetate.** A sheet of colored acetate, such as that used for report covers, placed over a printed page will darken the print and heighten the contrast of the print with the background paper for some students. Although available in other colors, yellow acetate provides effective contrast for most students. Be sure to use acetate that has a "dull" finish because shiny acetate sheets produce a great deal of glare.

- **Lamps.** Lamps with adjustable arms and controls to vary the intensity of light can provide the additional or dimmed illumination that a visually impaired student may require. Focusing a strong light directly on the student's reading material and trying different types of lighting (like halogen, incandescent, or full-spectrum bulbs) may improve a student's ability to see print material more clearly.

- **Large-print books.** Large-print books and materials that some students with low vision may need can be obtained commercially or by using the enlarging feature on a photocopy machine to make larger copies. The quality and size of the print, the typeface, and the spacing between letter and lines are all important considerations for legibility, however, so not all photoenlarged materials will be adequate for some students. In addition, it is often preferable for students to use optical devices with regular-print books, when possible, because the use of optical devices also provides access to the rest of the visual environment. Using such devices also reduces students' dependence on others to provide special materials.

- **Bold-line paper.** For students who find it difficult to see the lines on regular writing paper, bold-line paper is available in various formats, including graph paper, large-print staffs for music notation, and writing paper. The amount of white space between the lines can also vary to accommodate larger printing by a student with low vision.

- **Line markers and reading windows.** Devices that can be placed over print to isolate a single line or word may be especially helpful to students who find it difficult to focus on a word or track a line of print.

- **Sun visors and other shields.** Students who are light sensitive (photophobic) may need to block out some of the light and glare around them. Seat a light-sensitive student with his or her back toward the window and in a position that will eliminate reflections off the dry erase board or other smooth surfaces. A hat or visor may also help reduce glare and visual discomfort, as may putting dark construction paper over the student's desk or other shiny surfaces nearby.

- **Measurement tools.** Because standard rulers may be difficult for some visually impaired students to see, you may wish to substitute a yardstick or a ruler with fewer increments for the visually impaired student to use during class. Adapted measurement tools may be provided by the teacher of visually impaired students and are available in special catalogs.

- **Additional tools**. Many other adaptations are readily available, like calculators (including scientific calculators) with large displays and keys with large print, nonglare paper, and highlighters, that may help some students.

Devices for Enhancing Tactile Functioning

Students who have significant limitations in the amount of vision they can use will rely more on their other senses, such as touch, for tasks in school.

- **Braille.** Students who cannot use printed material for reading or who are totally blind may read braille, a code consisting of combinations of raised dots arranged in six-dot "cells" that represent the letters of the alphabet, numbers, and punctuation marks. Some students may be taught to read using braille and print simultaneously.

- **Tactile graphics.** Graphic images, such as pictures, graphs, charts, maps, and globes, that students cannot see are available in or can be made into tactile formats that they can explore with their fingers.

- **Braillewriter.** A braillewriter is a manually operated, six-key machine that, as its name indicates, is used to produce braille. The most popular model is the Perkins Brailler. Electronic braillewriters and computerized braille notetakers are also commonly used by students (see "Assistive Technology Devices").

- **Slate and stylus.** The slate and stylus is a portable, lightweight device used to write braille. The slate is a frame in which paper can be inserted. It has rows of small holes arranged in the shape of braille cells. The pointed stylus is used to poke through the holes, creating or "embossing" raised braille dots onto the paper. A slate and stylus can be easily carried in a pocket or on a clipboard.

- **Raised-line paper.** Raised-line paper, on which the lines are embossed to allow students to feel the lines that others see, comes in various formats. Raised-line writing paper allows a student to write script on the

Writing on a Perkins brailler.

line. Graph paper allows a student to construct a graph either by placing markers on the paper or by punching holes to indicate specific points.

- **Templates and writing guides.** Made out of cardboard, plastic, or metal, templates and writing guides are rectangular forms of various sizes with a space cut out to allow signatures or other information to be written within their boundaries. Many blind people use such guides to sign their names or write checks.

- **Raised-line drawing boards and other tactile writing devices.** A raised-line drawing board is a rubber-covered board on which a sheet of acetate is placed. When someone draws or writes on the acetate with a pen or other pointed object, it produces raised lines that can be felt. This device can be used to produce geometric shapes, script letters, or other line diagrams for students who cannot perceive them visually. Such drawings need to be presented in simple form, however, to be understood tactile-

A slate and stylus.

ly. Another device, a Thermo-pen, creates raised tactile writing on special heat-sensitive paper (as with any device that uses heat, it should be used only under supervision).

- **Raised marks.** Special markers, adhesive-backed materials, and glues that leave raised marks may be used to create lines or dots that can be easily felt. These raised markings can be used to mark regular intervals or the most commonly used settings on standard dials, measurement tools, and other objects. The markings made should be few and simple so that they can be easily identified.

- **Braille labeler.** Like print label makers, braille labelers produce braille on self-adhesive plastic or magnetic tape that can then be used to identify books, clothing, and other objects. Even people who do not know braille can easily use this tool to braille all the letters of the alphabet, numbers, and some braille contractions and punctuation marks. These labels work well on a variety of personal items, such as CDs and tapes, and enable students to be independent in organizing and using their own materials.

- **Measurement tools with braille and raised markings.** Various braille clocks, rulers, and measuring kits are specially designed for use by visually impaired students. The teacher of students with visual impairments can help locate this equipment, which can also be found in specialized catalogs.

- **Abacus.** The Cranmer abacus was especially adapted for blind individuals to facilitate mathematical computation. Teachers of visually impaired students instruct some students in its use and can discuss with you how to incorporate a student's use of the device into the regular classroom.

- **Teacher-made materials.** Teacher-made materials can provide visually impaired students with a rich source of unique tactile experiences that can enhance learning through touch and offer an opportunity for teachers to be creative. For example, young students enjoy books enhanced with a variety of tactile materials to represent the images and concepts in the story. Storybook bags can also be created, containing small objects that represent items, events, or concepts in the story.

- **Additional tactile materials and tools.** Stickers that can be used as rewards are available in tactile (as well as "scratch-and-sniff") formats. A variety of common objects and recreational materials are available in a tactile format, such as braille watches, clothing labels, playing cards, and board games.

Devices for Enhancing Auditory Functioning

Using devices that are equipped with sound can give visually impaired students access to information and help them perform their schoolwork. Such devices may be either everyday equipment or specialized products for people with visual impairments.

- **Cassette tape recorders.** Students may use a tape recorder for listening to recorded texts and other class-work, formulating compositions or writing assignments, and many other purposes.

- **Talking Books, recorded books, and e-books.** The Library of Congress National Library Service for the Blind and Physically Handicapped Talking Book program, Recording for the Blind and Dyslexic, and other organizations provide free library services to visually impaired persons. They offer a wide variety of texts and leisure-reading materials on Talking Book disks, cassette tapes, and computer disks for computers with speech synthesizers (see the next section on "Assistive Technology Devices"). Because the speeds at which the Talking Book disks and cassettes are played differ from the speeds of commercially manufactured recordings, the National Library Service also lends special Talking Book machines and cassette-playback machines to eligible persons. Portable cassette equipment that also records can be purchased from the American Printing House for the Blind and various other companies throughout the United States. (See Organizations of Interest to Teachers at the end of this booklet for addresses.)

- **Talking calculators.** Relatively inexpensive handheld talking calculators are available from several manufacturers. These devices "speak" each entry and result aloud and are capable of performing all computations. Earphones are available for many models. Talking scientific calculators with more advanced functions are also available but are more expensive.

- **Voice organizers and recorders**. A variety of commercially available recording devices can be used to record short notes and messages that can be played at a later time.

71

- **Audible gym equipment.** Adapted gym equipment, such as beeper balls and goal locators that emit beeps or other sounds, can be obtained by consulting with the teacher of students who are visually impaired. Planning ahead is essential because it may take time to order and purchase this equipment.

- **Additional auditory devices.** Many additional auditory devices, like talking watches, alarm clocks, thermometers, and money identifiers, are available for visually impaired students.

Assistive Technology Devices

In the field of visual impairment, *assistive technology* (also known as *adaptive* or *access technology*) usually refers to equipment, devices, and methods that provide access to the environment and print information for people with visual impairments using computer hardware and software and other electronic equipment. Rapid advances in this technology are increasing access to information and students' ability to complete school assignments independently.

The tools and devices listed here are some examples of the types of assistive technology that are available to students. Some allow the user to have access to information displayed on a computer screen and to use regular computer programs, while others are specialized tools to be used on their own.

- **CCTV.** A CCTV system uses a video camera to project an image onto a television screen or computer monitor. The student controls the size of the projected image and other features, including brightness and contrast. A student can use a CCTV to read regular-print books and maps at greatly enlarged sizes, as well as to do written assignments using a pen, pencil, or computer. CCTVs vary in styles and features, such as black-and-white or color images, built-in screens, handheld cameras, the ability to interface with a computer (such CCTVs are

72

known as *video magnifiers*), and the ability to focus on distant objects. Many CCTVs used in schools are fairly large and are usually stationary, but smaller, more portable models are increasingly becoming available.

- **Braille translation software.** Braille translation software converts print into braille (forward translation) and braille into print (back translation), enabling students to output braille translations of text from the computer for themselves and print versions of their written braille work for their teachers.

- **Braille printer.** A electronic braille printer (also called an embosser) connects to a computer and embosses braille on paper to provide hard-copy braille. It functions like a print printer.

- **Synthetic speech.** Using a combination of screen-reading software and a speech synthesizer, a visually impaired student can have access to what is presented on the computer screen. The screen reader converts the characters or words into spoken language, while the synthesizer produces the sound (either through the computer's speaker or a separate speaker). The user can control the speed of the speech as well as navigate the screen.

- **Screen-enlargement software.** Screen-enlargement software increases the size of images on computer screens.

- **Refreshable braille displays.** A refreshable braille display is an output device that is connected to a computer, often in front of or under the keyboard, on which characters can be felt in braille. The braille display consists of pins arranged in the shape of braille cells that raise and lower to form braille characters. Software converts the characters from the computer into the braille displayed on the refreshable display. Some portable notetakers also feature refreshable braille output.

- **Audible and braille notetakers.** Notetakers provide some of the capabilities of computers in a small portable device. They offer a variety of software and hardware functions and features such as synthetic speech output, refreshable braille, choice of keyboards (braille or standard), and braille translation. Notetakers can usually interface with a regular computer.

- **Electronic braillewriter.** An electronic braillewriter is a device that produces braille but also has special functions like synthetic speech, braille and print translation, automatic erase and correction, and a memory for storing files and can interface with a computer.

- **Optical character recognition (OCR) with speech and scanner.** OCR devices convert printed text into electronic files and serve as reading machines for visually impaired users. These devices use a scanner to input text and OCR software to convert the text into an electronic format that the user can then access in a variety of formats, such as braille or synthetic speech.

- **Tactile graphics maker.** A tactile graphics maker is a device that enables the automatic production of tactile graphic material using heat-sensitive paper.

The various devices that are available for visually impaired students to use are essential in helping students function in the classroom, complete their schoolwork, and get the most out of their education. Another critical factor in their success in school, however, is the support they receive from the people with whom they interact every day. Using the information and suggestions in this booklet, you can begin to create a warm, welcoming, and supportive atmosphere in your classroom for your student who is visually impaired that can help make your work together satisfying and successful.

APPENDIX A
Common Visual Impairments

The following are some of the common causes of visual impairments. You are likely to come across some of these terms in a student's records or in discussions with other members of the educational team. Understanding the causes and symptoms of your student's visual condition will make it easier to understand his or her special needs.

Albinism. A hereditary condition resulting in reduced visual acuity and in which there is a lack of pigment in the eyes or throughout the body. It is usually accompanied by nystagmus (*see* Nystagmus). People with albinism are sensitive to light and sometimes wear tinted eyeglasses indoors as well as outdoors. Because glare is particularly disturbing to them, these students usually prefer to sit away from windows. Placing a piece of black construction paper on a bright or shiny desk surface is also helpful in reducing glare.

Amblyopia. Reduced vision without observable changes in the structure of the eye. (For example, when there is a muscle imbalance, called strabismus, that may result in double vision [*see* Strabismus] the brain may suppress vision in one eye in an effort to resolve the problem.) The loss of vision is often permanent. This condition is particularly significant when vision in the other eye is adversely affected by other causes.

Astigmatism. Blurred vision caused by an irregular curvature of the eye. As a result of the irregular curvature, light rays are not sharply focused on the retina. A student with this condition may become restless or irritable when working for extended periods. The student may also tilt his or her head or change posture to maximize vision. Copying from the chalkboard or other activities that require frequent refocusing from far to near distance, or vice versa, may be particularly troublesome.

Cataract. A condition in which the normally transparent lens of the eye becomes cloudy or opaque. Usually a student with this condition is sensitive to light and glare and may squint to keep extraneous light from entering the eye. Students with cataracts usually have the lens removed and replaced with an artificial lens.

Cortical visual impairment. A visual impairment caused by dysfunction in the systems of the brain related to vision, such as the visual pathway or the occipital lobes of the brain. The degree of visual impairment can vary greatly, even from day to day, and the individual may not consistently understand or interpret what the eye sees. Cortical visual impairment is common in students who have other disabilities caused by neurological dysfunction.

Glaucoma. A condition in which pressure of the fluid inside the eye is too high. Depending on the type of glaucoma, visual loss may be gradual, sudden, or present at birth. When visual loss is gradual, it begins with decreasing peripheral vision. If medication is prescribed to control the pressure and to prevent further damage to the eye, the student with glaucoma should be encouraged to take it regularly.

Hyperopia (farsightedness). A condition that is usually caused by the eyeball's being too short from front to back, which results in farsightedness. Close objects appear out of focus to students with this condition, who may find it difficult to do work at their desks for extended periods.

Macular degeneration. A condition resulting in reduced acuity and a blind spot in the central portion of the visual field (the macula). Students with this condition have good peripheral and movement vision but have difficulty with work that requires good detail vision, such as reading and handwriting practice. Although macular degeneration is most often a disease of older adults, most children with macular degeneration have Stargardt's disease, a hereditary condition.

Myopia (nearsightedness). A condition usually caused by the eyeball being too long from front to back. People with this condition can see nearby objects clearly, but distant objects appear out of focus. Using a worksheet and doing other close work may be easier for these students than may copying from the chalkboard.

Nystagmus. A condition that involves small, involuntary, rapid movements of the eyeballs from side to side, in a rotary or pendular motion or in a combination of these movements. Students with this condition may lose their place frequently when reading. Placing a cutout reading window or line marker over the reading material is helpful in alleviating this problem.

Optic atrophy. Degeneration of the optic nerve causing reduced visual acuity. In general, students with this condition hold reading material close to their eyes and prefer bright light. They may also display variable visual ability throughout the day and from day to day.

Optic nerve hypoplasia. Underdevelopment of the optic nerve, which may produce a wide range of visual functioning, from normal visual acuity to no light perception.

Retinitis pigmentosa. A hereditary degeneration of the retina that begins with night blindness and produces a gradual loss of peripheral vision. Although some people with this disease lose all their vision in adulthood, many retain some central vision with normal or reduced visual acuity. Regular-print materials are generally better than are large-print materials for these students. Travel in crowds or unfamiliar areas may be difficult because persons, objects, or obstacles in the periphery of vision (on the sides, above, or below) are not seen.

Retinopathy of prematurity. A condition often found in infants with low birth weight, resulting in reduced visual acuity or total blindness. It is usually associated with other disabilities. Retinopathy of prematurity was formerly called retrolental fibroplasia and was found in premature infants who were given oxygen during incubation.

Strabismus. A condition in which the eyes are not simultaneously directed to the same object as a result of an imbalance of the muscles of the eyeball.

APPENDIX B
Organizations of Interest to Teachers

Your most valuable resources for additional information about visual impairment that you, your student, or the student's family may need are the teacher of visually impaired students and the O&M instructor who are assigned to your school. These specialists are familiar with national and local groups dedicated to serving visually impaired students in your area if you need to consult them regarding services, referrals, or further information. In addition, the organizations listed in this appendix are primary sources of information and referral and are a good place to start to find answers to any questions about visual impairment, services for people who are visually impaired, and ways to assist your student and his or her family. The *AFB Directory of Services for Blind and Visually Impaired Persons in the United States and Canada*, published by the American Foundation for the Blind and found in many libraries, offers more comprehensive listings of organizations and services and volunteer groups in your state and nationwide. It can also be searched electronically at the AFB web site, www.afb.org.

American Council of the Blind
1155 15th Street, NW, Suite 1004
Washington, DC 20005
phone: 202-467-5081 or 800-424-8666
fax: 202-467-5085
e-mail: info@acb.org
web site: www.acb.org

A national clearinghouse for information, the council promotes the effective participation of blind people in all aspects of society. It provides information and referral; legal assistance and representation; scholarships; leadership and legislative training; consumer advocate support; assistance in technological research; a speaker referral service; consultative and advisory services to individuals, organizations, and agencies; and assistance with developing programs.

American Foundation for the Blind
11 Penn Plaza, Suite 300
New York, NY 10001
phone: 212-502-7600 or 800-232-5463 (800-AFB-LINE)
fax: 212-502-7777
e-mail: afbinfo@afb.net
web site: www.afb.org

This national organization provides services to and acts as an information clearinghouse for people who are visually impaired and their families, the public, professionals, schools, organizations, and corporations. It conducts research and mounts program initiatives to promote the inclusion of visually impaired persons, including the National Literacy Center and the National Technology Program; advocates for services and legislation; and maintains the M. C. Migel Memorial Library and the Helen Keller Archives. AFB maintains offices in Atlanta; Chicago; Dallas; Huntington, West Virginia; and San Francisco and a governmental relations office in Washington, DC. It produces videos and publishes books, pamphlets, the *Directory of Services for Blind and Visually Impaired Persons in the United States and Canada*, the *Journal of Visual Impairment & Blindness*, and *AccessWorld*. In addition, it provides information about the latest technology available for visually impaired persons through its National Technology Program and operates a toll-free information hotline.

American Printing House for the Blind
1839 Frankfort Avenue
Louisville, KY 40206
phone: 502-895-2405 or 800-223-1839
fax: 502-899-2274
e-mail: info@aph.org
web site: www.aph.org

This national organization receives an annual appropriation from Congress to provide textbooks and educational aids for legally blind students who attend elementary and secondary schools or special educational institutions. It produces a wide variety of books and learning materials in braille and other media and manufactures computer-access equipment, software, and special education and reading devices for visually impaired persons. The organization maintains an educational research and development program and a reference catalog database providing information about textbooks and other materials that are produced in accessible media.

Association for Education and Rehabilitation of the Blind and Visually Impaired
4600 Duke Street, Suite 430
Alexandria, VA 22304
phone: 703-823-9690 or 877-492-2708
fax: 703-823-9695
e-mail: aer@aerbvi.org
web site: www.aerbvi.org

AER serves as the membership organization for professionals who work in all phases of education and rehabilitation with visually impaired persons of all ages on the local, regional, national, and international levels. It seeks to develop and promote professional excellence through such support services as continuing education, publications, information dissemination, lobbying and advocacy, and conferences and workshops.

Council for Exceptional Children Division on Visual Impairments
1110 North Glebe Road, Suite 300
Arlington, VA 22201-5704
phone: 703-620-3660 or 888-CEC-SPED
TTY (text only): 703-264-9446
fax: 703-264-9494
e-mail: service@cec.sped.org
web site: www.cec.sped.org
www.ed.arizona.edu/dvi (Division on Visual Impairments)

CEC is a professional organization of teachers, school administrators, and others who are concerned with children who require special services. It publishes periodicals, books, and other materials on teaching exceptional children, advocates for appropriate government policies, provides professionals development, and disseminates information on effective instructional strategies. The Division on Visual Impairments focuses on the education of children who are visually impaired and the concerns of professionals who work with them.

Howe Press of the Perkins School for the Blind
175 North Beacon Street
Watertown, MA 02171
phone: 617-924-3400
fax: 617-926-2027
e-mail: HowePress@perkins.put.kas.ma.us
web site: www.perkins.pvt.k12.ma.us/brailler.htm

Howe Press manufactures and sells a variety of products for visually impaired persons, including the Perkins Brailler (manual or electric); slates; styli; mathematical aids; braille games; braille-vision books for children; heavy- and light-grade braille paper; and Tactile Drawing Kits.

National Association for Parents of Children with Visual Impairments
P.O. Box 317
Watertown, MA 02272-0317
phone: 617-972-7444 or 800-562-6265
fax: (617) 972-7444
web site: www.napvi.org

This membership association supports state and local parents' groups and conducts advocacy workshops for parents of visually impaired children and youths. In addition, it operates a national clearinghouse for information, education, and referral; fosters communication among federal, state, and local agencies that provide services or funding for services; and promotes public understanding of the needs and rights of visually impaired children and youths.

82

National Braille Press

88 St. Stephen Street
Boston, MA 02115
phone: 617-266-6160 or 888-965-8965
fax: 617-437-0456
e-mail: orders@nbp.org
web site: www.nbp.org

The National Braille Press provides braille printing
services for publishers and other organizations,
including the Library of Congress; offers transcription of
documents related to school or work; and sponsors a
children's Braille Book-of the-Month Club.

National Federation of the Blind

1800 Johnson Street
Baltimore, MD 21230
phone: 410-659-9314
fax: 410-685-5653
e-mail: nfb@nfb.org
web site: www.nfb.org

The federation, with affiliates in all states and the
District of Columbia, works to improve the social and
economic conditions of visually impaired persons. It
evaluates programs and provides assistance in
establishing new ones, grants scholarships to people
who are visually impaired, and conducts a public
education program. It also publishes *The Braille Monitor*
and *Future Reflections,* a magazine for parents.

National Library Service for the Blind
and Physically Handicapped
Library of Congress

1291 Taylor Street, NW
Washington, DC 20542
phone: 202-707-5100 or 800-424-8567
TDD: 202-707-0744
fax: 202-707-0712
e-mail: nls@loc.gov
web site: www.loc.gov/nls

The National Library Service for the Blind and
Physically Handicapped conducts a national program to
distribute free reading materials—classics, current

fiction, and general nonfiction—in braille and on recorded disks and cassettes to visually and physically handicapped persons who cannot utilize ordinary printed materials. Materials are distributed and playback equipment is lent free of charge through a network of regional and subregional libraries and machine-lending agencies. In addition, the service operates a reference information section on all aspects of blindness and other physical disabilities that affect reading. It functions as a bibliographic center on reading materials for people with disabilities and organizations that lend reading materials in special media.

Prevent Blindness America
500 East Remington Road
Schaumburg, IL 60173
phone: 847-843-2020 or 800-331-2020
fax: 847-843-8458
e-mail: info@preventblindness.org
web site: www.preventblindness.org

Through state affiliates, the society conducts a program of public and professional education, research, and industrial and community services to prevent blindness. Its services include the promotion and support of local glaucoma screening programs, preschool vision testing, industrial eye safety, the collection of data on the nature and extent of the causes of blindness and low vision, the improvement of environmental conditions affecting eye health in schools and colleges, and the dissemination of information on low vision devices and clinics.

Recording for the Blind and Dyslexic
20 Roszel Road
Princeton, NJ 08540
(609) 452-0606 (local, toll-free) or (800) 883-7201
E-mail: custserv@rfbd.org
www.rfbd.org

This organization lends recorded and electronic materials and textbooks at no charge to people who cannot read standard print because of visual, physical, or learning disabilities.

APPENDIX C
Suggestions for Further Reading and Reference

Corn, A. L., Cowan, C. M., & Moses, E. (1988). *You seem like a regular kid to me* (pamphlet). New York: American Foundation for the Blind.

D'Andrea, F. M., & Farrenkopf, C. (2000). *Looking to learn: Promoting literacy for students with low vision.* New York: AFB Press.

Dodson-Burke, B., & Hill, E. W. (1989). *An orientation and mobility primer for young children and their families.* New York: American Foundation for the Blind.

Holbrook, M. C. (Ed.). (1996). *Children with visual impairments: A parent's guide.* Bethesda, MD: Woodbine House.

Holbrook, M. C., & Koenig, A. J. (Eds.). (2000). *Foundations of education* (2nd ed). Vol. 1: *History and theory of teaching children and youths with visual impairments.* Vol. 2: *Instructional Strategies for teaching children and youths with visual impairments.* New York: AFB Press.

Lewis, S., & Allman, C. B. (2000). *Seeing eye to eye: An administrator's guide to students with low vision.* New York: AFB Press.

Longuil, C. (1991). *Oh I see!* (video). New York: American Foundation for the Blind.

Low vision questions and answers: Definitions, devices, services (pamphlet). (1987). New York: American Foundation for the Blind.

The new what do you do when you see a blind person? (video). (2000). New York: AFB Press.

Pugh, G. S., & Erin, J. (Eds.). (1999). *Blind and visually impaired students: Educational service guidelines.* Watertown, MA: Perkins School for the Blind in cooperation with the National Association of State Directors of Special Education.

Wormsley, D. P., & D'Andrea, F. M. (Eds.). (1997). *Instructional strategies for braille literacy.* New York: AFB Press.

About the Contributors

Susan J. Spungin, Ed.D., is Vice President, Educational and International Programs, American Foundation for the Blind, New York, New York.

Donna McNear, M.A., is a teacher for students with visual impairments and certified orientation and mobility specialist, Rum River Special Education Cooperative, Cambridge, Minnesota.

Iris Torres, M.A., is Technology Trainer, Technology Solutions, District 75, New York City Public Schools, New York.

Anne L. Corn, Ed.D., is Professor of Special Education, Ophthalmology, and Visual Sciences at Vanderbilt University, Nashville, Tennessee.

Jane Erin, Ph.D., is Associate Professor and Director of Programs in Visual Impairment in the Department of Special Education, Rehabilitation, and School Psychology at the University of Arizona at Tucson.

Carol Farrenkopf, Ed.D., is Special Education Consultant (Low Incidence) for the Toronto District School Board, and Instructor, Teacher Preparation Program (Visual Impairment), College of Education, at the University of Western Ontario in London, Ontario, Canada.

Kathleen Mary Huebner, Ph.D., is Associate Dean, Graduate Studies in Vision Impairment of the Institute for the Visually Impaired at the Pennsylvania College of Optometry, Elkins Park, Pennsylvania.